DAILY WORDS

WORDS

CLAIMING A PROMISE
for every day of the year

COMPILED BY
ROBERT BACKHOUSE

Revell

Fleming H. Revell Company
Publishers
Old Tappan, New Jersey

CONTENTS

JANUARY
Beginnings

FEBRUARY
The Battle

MARCH
Jesus' Cross

CONTENTS

APRIL
Jesus' Resurrection

MAY
Renewal

JUNE
Fellowship

CONTENTS

JULY
Jesus' Promises

AUGUST
God's Refreshment

SEPTEMBER
Giving Thanks to God

CONTENTS

OCTOBER
Bearing Fruit

NOVEMBER
Jesus' Second Coming

DECEMBER
Jesus' First Coming

Introduction

Here are 366 Bible promises and assurances of God's love
— one for every day of the year. These promises are
grouped together in two ways in this book. First, they are
linked to the seasons: so January has "Beginnings" for the
New Year, and September has "Giving Thanks to God"
with Harvest in mind. Second, the promises have been
selected to fit in with the Christian Year, so that March and
April, about the time of Easter, have promises about the
cross of Jesus and his resurrection; May, usually the time
for celebrating Pentecost, has promises about the work of
the Holy Spirit; and then, of course, December is given
over to Christmas. By using this book daily we will become
familiar with what God has so wonderfully promised to do
in the lives of his followers.

Until God's promises are collected together in a book like
this we may not be fully aware of how many promises the
Bible contains, or the wide variety of subjects they cover.
But this book was not meant to be simply a source of
interesting information. It is hoped that as you read God's
Word in this way each day you will meet with the living
God who made these promises. A preacher from the last
century advised: "Take each promise of God, one by one,
put it under your tongue, and eat it slowly as if it were
your favorite dessert." This is what people mean when
they talk about "meditating" on God's Word. What we are
invited to do each day is to read God's promise, and to
humbly take it with us into our hearts and lives so that it
stays with us throughout the day. Some people find that
the best way to do this is to read the promise over several
times at different moments during the day, while others

memorize the verse, or part of the verse, and bring it to mind during the day, thanking God for his promises.

The Psalmist wrote that he loved to meditate on God's instructions and precepts. In Psalm 119, verses 147 and 148, he went as far as to say: "I rise before dawn and cry for help; I have put my hope in your word. My eyes stay open through the watches of the night, that I may meditate on your promises." No wonder he was also able to write: "Your word is a lamp to my feet and a light to my path" (verse 105). May you also, as you read God's promises, discover this to be true.

Beginnings

For many the New Year can be a time for sad reflection and bitter resentment about the past. Others are swamped by a sense of despair as they peer with foreboding into the future.

Yet God has said, "Behold, I make all things new." Who wouldn't like to have a new vision, a new life, a new hope and a new direction as they set out on the New Year? It is possible for us all to experience this as we put our hand in the hand of Jesus Christ and travel with him through each day of this New Year.

God is the God of new beginnings. So, no matter how sinful, unfaithful to God or unkind to other people we may have been in the year that has just passed, God offers us forgiveness and a fresh start with him at the beginning of this New Year.

JANUARY

New Vision

—— *1st* ——

God said to Noah, "I have set my rainbow in the
clouds, and it will be the sign of the covenant between me and the
earth."   GENESIS 9.13

—— *2nd* ——

As far as the east is from the west, so far has God
removed our transgressions from us.   PSALM 103.12

—— *3rd* ——

I will instruct you and teach you in the way you
should go; I will counsel you and watch over you.   PSALM 32.8

—— *4th* ——

"Though your sins are like scarlet, they shall be as
white as snow; though they are red as crimson, they shall be like
wool."   ISAIAH 1.18

—— *5th* ——

The Lord's compassions never fail. They are new
every morning.   LAMENTATIONS 3.22–23

—— *6th* ——

Christ is the mediator of the new covenant, that those
who are called may receive the promised eternal inheritance.
HEBREWS 9.15

—— *7th* ——

He who was seated on the throne said, "I am making
everything new."   REVELATION 21.5

New Life

—— *8th* ——

God has given us eternal life, and this life is in his
Son. He who has the Son has life.   1 JOHN 5.11–12

—— *9th* ——

"I will give you a new heart and put a new spirit
within you."   EZEKIEL 36.26

—— *10th* ——

"I am the living bread that came down from heaven.
If anyone eats of this bread, he will live forever."   JOHN 6.51

—— *11th* ——

If anyone is in Christ, he is a new creation; the old has
gone, the new has come!   2 CORINTHIANS 5.17

—— *12th* ——

"My dwelling place will be with them; I will be their
God, and they will be my people."   EZEKIEL 37.27

—— *13th* ——

"The Son of Man did not come to be served, but to
serve, and to give his life as a ransom for many."   MATTHEW 20.28

—— *14th* ——

"Everyone who believes in [the Son of Man] may have
eternal life."   JOHN 3.15

JANUARY

New Hope

—— *15th* ——

For great is your love, higher than the heavens;
your faithfulness reaches to the skies.   PSALM 108.4

—— *16th* ——

In God's great mercy he has given us new birth into a
living hope through the resurrection of Jesus Christ from
the dead.   1 PETER 1.3

—— *17th* ——

Everlasting joy will crown their heads. Gladness and
joy will overtake them, and sorrow and sighing will flee away.
ISAIAH 35.10

—— *18th* ——

His kingdom is an eternal kingdom; his dominion
endures from generation to generation.   DANIEL 4.3

—— *19th* ——

"[God] will wipe away every tear from their eyes.
There will be no more death or mourning or crying or pain, for
the old order of things has passed away."   REVELATION 21.4

——*20th* ——

"Come to me, all of you who are weary and burdened,
and I will give you rest."   MATTHEW 11.28

——*21st*——

In keeping with God's promises we are looking
forward to a new heaven and a new earth, the home of
righteousness.   1 PETER 3.13

JANUARY

New Direction

——— 22nd ———

God, who has called you into fellowship with his Son
Jesus Christ our Lord, is faithful.   1 CORINTHIANS 1.9

——— 23rd ———

The word of the Lord came to Abram in a vision: "Do
not be afraid, Abram. I am your shield, your very great reward."
GENESIS 15.1

——— 24th ———

God said to Joshua, "Do not be discouraged, for the
Lord your God will be with you wherever you go."   JOSHUA 1.9

——— 25th ———

"Before I formed you in the womb I knew you,
before you were born I set you apart; I appointed you as a
prophet to the nations."   JEREMIAH 1.5

——— 26th ———

"Come, follow me," Jesus said to Simon and Andrew,
"and I will make you fishers of men."   MARK 1.17

——— 27th ———

"You will be his witness to all men of what you have
seen and heard."   ACTS 22.15

——— 28th ———

The one who calls you is faithful and he will do it.
1 THESSALONIANS 5.24

JANUARY

——— *29th* ———

Just as Christ was raised from the dead through the
glory of the Father, we too may live a new life.   ROMANS 6.4

——— *30th* ———

O Lord, you are our Father. We are the clay, you are
the potter; we are all the work of your hand.   ISAIAH 64.8

——— *31st* ———

We have been released from the law so that we serve
in the new way of the Spirit, and not in the old way of the written
code.   ROMANS 7.6

FEBRUARY

The Battle

It's not just that the Christian life has its ups and downs. It's more
than that: it's a battle. Every saint testifies to the fact that the
closer we are drawn to God, the more keenly we feel our own
sinfulness. Jesus Christ himself had fight after fight with the
devil. Who other than the devil was behind the taunt that was
flung at Jesus in his dying hour of agony, "If you are the Son of
God come down from the cross"?
In *Pilgrim's Progress*, John Bunyan graphically portrays Christian
languishing in Doubting Castle where he is about to be killed by
Giant Despair. But Christian discovers a key called Promise and
so escapes from the castle and the clutches of the giant. In the
same way, the Bible promises set out here for February can help
us in our spiritual battles. As we resist the devil, fight against
temptation, fend off all kinds of evil attacks and wrestle in
prayer, God's promises open the door to freedom and victory.

The Battle Against the Devil

——— *1st* ———

Be self-controlled and alert. Your enemy the devil
prowls around like a roaring lion looking for someone to devour.
1 PETER 5.8

———*2nd* ———

Put on the full armor of God so that you can take your
stand against the devil's schemes.   EPHESIANS 6.11

———*3rd* ———

Submit yourselves, then, to God. Resist the devil, and
he will flee from you.   JAMES 4.7

——— *4th* ———

Since the children have flesh and blood, [Jesus] too
shared in their humanity so that by his death he might destroy
him who holds the power of death—that is, the devil.
HEBREWS 2.14

——— *5th* ———

The God of peace will soon crush Satan under your
feet.   ROMANS 16.20

——— *6th* ———

The Lord is faithful and he will strengthen and protect
you from the evil one.   2 THESSALONIANS 3.3

——— *7th* ———

"I am sending you to open their eyes and turn them
from darkness to light, and from the power of Satan to God, so
that they may receive forgiveness of sins and a place among those
who are sanctified by faith in me."   ACTS 26.17–18

The Battle Against Temptation and Sin

—— *8th* ——

Through Christ Jesus the law of the Spirit of life set me free from the law of sin and death.   ROMANS 8.2

—— *9th* ——

Those controlled by their sinful nature cannot please God. You, however, are controlled not by your sinful nature but by the Spirit.   ROMANS 8.8–9

—— *10th* ——

If through the power of the Holy Spirit you crush [your old sinful nature] and its evil deeds, you shall live.   ROMANS 8.13

—— *11th* ——

In your struggle against sin, you have not yet resisted to the point of shedding your blood.... Endure hardship as discipline; God is treating you as sons. For what son is not disciplined by his father?   HEBREWS 12.4,7

—— *12th* ——

Consider [Jesus] who endured such opposition from sinful men, so that you will not grow weary.   HEBREWS 12.3

—— *13th* ——

Here is a trustworthy saying: ... if we are faithless, [Christ] will remain faithful.   2 TIMOTHY 2.11,13

—— *14th* ——

No temptation has seized you except what is common to man. And God is faithful; he will not let you be tempted beyond what you can bear. But when you are tempted, he will also provide a way out so that you can stand up under it.
1 CORINTHIANS 10.13

Trials and Persecution

—— *15th* ——

Consider it pure joy, my brothers, whenever you face
trials of many kinds, because you know that the testing of your
faith develops perseverance.   JAMES 1.2–3

—— *16th* ——

"Blessed are you when people insult you, persecute you and
falsely say all kinds of evil against you because of me. Rejoice and
be glad."   MATTHEW 5.11–12

—— *17th* ——

We also rejoice in our sufferings, because we know that
suffering produces perseverance; perseverance, character; and
character, hope.   ROMANS 5.3–4

—— *18th* ——

In this you greatly rejoice, though now for a little
while you may have suffered grief in all kinds of trials. These
have come so that your faith ... may be proved genuine and may
result in praise.   1 PETER 1.6–7

—— *19th* ——

We do not want you to become lazy, but to imitate
those who through faith and patience inherit what has been
promised.   HEBREWS 6.12

—— *20th* ——

"You will be betrayed by parents, brothers, relatives
and friends, and they will put some of you to death. All men will
hate you because of me. But not a hair of your head will perish.
By standing firm you will save yourselves."   LUKE 21.16–19

—— *21st* ——

I can do all things through [the Lord] who gives me
strength.   PHILIPPIANS 4.13

FEBRUARY

The Battle
Against Giving Up as a Christian

—— *22nd* ——

I press on toward the goal to win the prize for which
God has called me heavenward in Christ Jesus.   PHILIPPIANS 3.14

—— *23rd* ——

Do you not know that in a race all the runners run,
but only one gets the prize? Run in such a way as to get the prize.
1 CORINTHIANS 9.24

—— *24th* ——

Everyone who competes in the games goes into strict
training. They do it to get a crown of laurel that will not last; but
we do it to get a crown that will last forever.
1 CORINTHIANS 9.25,26

—— *25th* ——

And we know that in all things God works for the
good of those who love him, who have been called according to
his purpose.   ROMANS 8.28

—— *26th* ——

God's gifts and his call are irrevocable.   ROMANS 11.29

—— *27th* ——

God ... has saved us and called us to a holy life—not
because of anything we have done but because of his own
purpose and grace. This grace was given us in Christ Jesus before
the beginning of time.   2 TIMOTHY 1.8–9

—— *28th* ——

"Because of the increase of wickedness, the love of
most will grow cold, but he who stands firm to the end will be
saved."   MATTHEW 24.12–13

MARCH

Jesus' Cross

Jesus Christ was born to die. At his birth Jesus was presented with myrrh to remind us about his death. When Jesus was circumcised and given his name, Mary was told by the elderly Simeon that "a sword will pierce your own soul." As Mary watched Jesus die through the most painful method of execution devised by man, she realized how true Simeon's prophecy had been.

The death of Jesus is central to each of the four Gospel writers. In Mark's Gospel six out of his sixteen chapters are given over to the last week of Jesus' life.

Jesus himself predicted his own death on a number of occasions. He explained why he had to die when he said that the Son of Man came "to give his life as a ransom for many" (Mark 10.45). His own close followers did not understand the significance of his death until after his resurrection, even though the Old Testament law and prophets taught the purpose behind his death. Later, in their letters, the apostles explained how the cross of Christ demonstrated the length, height, depth and breadth of God's love.

Jesus' Cross Brings Forgiveness

—— *1st* ——

In [Christ] we have redemption through his blood,
the forgiveness of sins, in accordance with the riches of God's
grace.   EPHESIANS 1.7

—— *2nd* ——

For [God] has rescued us from the dominion of
darkness and brought us into the kingdom of the Son he loves, in
whom we have redemption, the forgiveness of sins.
COLOSSIANS 1.13–14

—— *3rd* ——

If we walk in the light, as [God] is in the light, we have
fellowship with one another, and the blood of Jesus, his Son,
purifies us from every sin.   1 JOHN 1.7

—— *4th* ——

God exalted [Jesus] to his own right hand as Prince
and Savior that he might give repentance and forgiveness of sins
to Israel.   ACTS 5.31

—— *5th* ——

[Christ] has appeared once for all at the end of the
ages to do away with sin by the sacrifice of himself.   HEBREWS 9.26

—— *6th* ——

For as far as the heavens are above the earth, so great
is his love for those who fear him; as far as the east is from the
west, so far has he removed our transgressions from us.
PSALM 103.11–12

—— *7th* ——

If we confess our sins, [God] is faithful and just and
will forgive us our sins and purify us from all unrighteousness.
1 JOHN 1.9

Jesus' Cross Offers Peace and Reconciliation

—— *8th* ——

Therefore, since we have been justified through
faith, we have peace with God through our Lord Jesus Christ.
ROMANS 5.1

—— *9th* ——

For [Christ] himself is our peace.   EPHESIANS 2.14

—— *10th* ——

For God was pleased to have all his fullness dwell in
[Christ], and through him ... making peace through his blood,
shed on the cross.   COLOSSIANS 1.19–20

—— *11th* ——

[Christ's] purpose was to create in himself one new
man ... thus making peace.   EPHESIANS 2.15

—— *12th* ——

For if, when we were God's enemies, we were
reconciled to him through the death of his Son, how much more,
having been reconciled, shall we be saved through his life!
ROMANS 5.10

—— *13th* ——

God ... reconciled us to himself through Christ and
gave us the ministry of reconciliation: that God was reconciling
the world to himself in Christ.   2 CORINTHIANS 5.18–19

—— *14th* ——

[Christ] came to preach peace to you who were far
away and peace to those who were near.   EPHESIANS 2.17

Jesus' Cross Demonstrates Love

—— *15th* ——

"For God so loved the world that he gave his one and
only Son, that whoever believes in him shall not perish but have
everlasting life." JOHN 3.16

—— *16th* ——

... so that Christ may dwell in your hearts through faith.
And I pray that you, being rooted and established in love, may
have power, together with all the saints, to grasp how wide and
long and high and deep is the love of Christ. EPHESIANS 3.17–18

—— *17th* ——

This is how God showed his love among us: He sent
his one and only Son into the world that we might live through
him. 1 JOHN 4.9

—— *18th* ——

Because of his great love for us, God, who is rich in
mercy, made us alive with Christ even when we were dead in
trangressions — it is by grace you have been saved.
EPHESIANS 2.4–5

—— *19th* ——

May our Lord Jesus Christ himself and God our
Father, who loved us and by his grace gave us eternal
encouragement and good hope, encourage and strengthen you
in every good deed and word. 2 THESSALONIANS 2.16–17

—— *20th* ——

God demonstrates his own love for us in this: While
we were still sinners, Christ died for us. ROMANS 5.8

—— *21st* ——

This is love: not that we loved God, but that he loved us
and sent his Son as an atoning sacrifice for our sins. 1 JOHN 4.10

Jesus' Cross Achieving Righteousness and Justification

—— *22nd* ——

To the man who does not work but trusts God who
justifies the wicked, his faith is credited as righteousness.
ROMANS 4.5

—— *23rd* ——

Christ Jesus ... our righteousness, holiness and redemption.
1 CORINTHIANS 1.30

—— *24th* ——

This righteousness from God comes through faith in
Jesus Christ to all who believe.   ROMANS 3.21–22

—— *25th* ——

We, too, have put our faith in Christ Jesus that we
may be justified by faith in Christ and not by observing the law,
because by observing the law no one will be justified.
GALATIANS 2.16–17

—— *26th* ——

"Through Jesus the forgiveness of sins is proclaimed
to you."   ACTS 13.38

—— *27th* ——

Clearly no one is justified before God by the law,
because, "The righteous will live by faith."   GALATIANS 3.11

—— *28th* ——

Those whom [God] predestined, he also called; those
he called, he also justified; those he justified, he also glorified.
ROMANS 8.30

—— *29th* ——

[One of the criminals] said, "Jesus, remember me
when you come into your kingdom." Jesus answered him, "I tell
you the truth, today you will be with me in paradise."

LUKE 23.42–43

—— *30th* ——

All ... are justified freely by [God's] grace through
the redemption that came by Christ Jesus. God presented him as
a sacrifice of atonement, through faith in his blood.

ROMANS 3.24–25

—— *31st* ——

For it is by grace that you have been saved, through
faith — and this not from yourselves, it is the gift of God—not by
works, so that no one can boast.   EPHESIANS 2.8–9

Jesus' Resurrection

On the first Easter Day, Jesus' followers doubted that Jesus Christ really had come alive. The significance of the resurrection of Jesus is that if Jesus had not risen it would have meant that he was sinful, that he was not the Savior of the world and that we are left to wallow in our sins.

When Peter entered the tomb where the body of Jesus had been placed, John 20.6–8 tells us, "He saw the strips of linen lying there, as well as the burial cloth that had been around Jesus' head. The cloth was folded up by itself, separate from the linen. Finally the other disciple, who had reached the tomb first, also went inside. He saw and believed".

John wants us to take note of the strips of linen lying there. Jesus' body was wrapped after his death in the same way that it had been wrapped after his birth. Swaddling clothes consist of a long bandage wound round and round a little baby's body. When a person was buried in Jesus' day a thirty-yard strip was wrapped round and round, from the shoulders, right down to the feet. A shorter bandage was wrapped round the head, from the eyebrows upwards, like a turban. The body was wrapped with just the face and the shoulders exposed, and then the body was laid in the tomb.

When Peter and John ran to the tomb they found that the bandages were wrapped round but collapsed, lying flat, except for the head-cloth, which had kept its shape. It was rolled up lying by itself, separated from the bandages. You can't get a body out of bandages without unravelling them. They would have been spread for yards, not only over the tomb floor, but out of the tomb into the garden. And yet, there they were, rolled up, and when John went in and saw them he knew that no man had been in the tomb. No man could have done it. No man could have got Jesus' body through those bandages. No wonder John saw and believed!

Jesus' Resurrection Foretold

—— *1st* ——

He will swallow up death for ever. The Sovereign
Lord will wipe away the tears from all faces; he will remove the
disgrace of his people from all the earth. The Lord has spoken.
ISAIAH 25.8

—— *2nd* ——

"The Son of Man is going to be betrayed into the
hands of men. They will kill him, and after three days he will
rise." MARK 9.31

—— *3rd* ——

"But about the resurrection of the dead, have you not
read what God said to you, 'I am the God of Abraham, the God
of Isaac, and the God of Jacob'? He is not the God of the dead but
of the living." MATTHEW 22.31–32

—— *4th* ——

Jesus said to [Martha], "I am the resurrection and the life.
He who believes in me will live, even though he dies." JOHN 11.25

—— *5th* ——

[Peter said,] "God has raised this Jesus to life, and we
are all wiktnesses of the fact." ACTS 2.32

—— *6th* ——

"For as Jonah was three days and three nights in the
belly of a huge fish, so the Son of Man will be three days and three
nights in the heart of the earth." MATTHEW 12.40

—— *7th* ——

The next day, the one after Preparation Day, the
chief priests and the Pharisees went to Pilate. "Sir," they said, "we
remember that while he was still alive that imposter said, 'After
three days I will rise again.'" MATTHEW 27.62–63

Jesus' Resurrection Transforms Death

—— *8th* ——

Christ has indeed been raised from the dead, the firstfruits of those who have fallen asleep.   1 CORINTHIANS 15.20

—— *9th* ——

I want to know Christ and the power of his resurrection and the fellowship of sharing in his sufferings, becoming like him in his death, and so, somehow, to attain to the resurrection from the dead.   PHILIPPIANS 3.10–11

—— *10th* ——

If we have been united with [Christ] in his death, we will certainly also be united with him in his resurrection.
ROMANS 6.5

—— *11th* ——

The body that is sown is perishable, it is raised imperishable; it is sown in dishonor, it is raised in glory; it is sown in weakness, it is raised in power.   1 CORINTHIANS 15.42–43

—— *12th* ——

We know that the one who raised the Lord Jesus from the dead will also raise us with Jesus.   2 CORINTHIANS 4.14

—— *13th* ——

Now if we died with Christ, we believe that we will also live with him. For we know that since Christ was raised from the dead, he can not die again; death no longer has mastery over him.
ROMANS 6.8–9

—— *14th* ——

For since death came through a man, the resurrection of the dead comes also through a man.   1 CORINTHIANS 15.21

Jesus' Resurrection Revolutionizes Individuals

───── *15th* ─────

[God] has given us new birth into a living hope through the resurrection of Jesus Christ from the dead.   1 PETER 1.3

───── *16th* ─────

In [the ark] only a few people, eight in all, were saved through water, and this water symbolizes baptism that now saves you also.... It saves you by the resurrection of Jesus Christ, who has gone into heaven and is at God's right hand.   1 PETER 3.20–22

───── *17th* ─────

Just as Christ was raised from the dead through the glory of the Father, we too may live a new life.   ROMANS 6.4

───── *18th* ─────

With great power the apostles continued to testify to the resurrection of the Lord Jesus, and much grace was with them.   ACTS 4.33

───── *19th* ─────

[Christ] was put to death in the body but made alive by the Spirit.   1 PETER 3.18

───── *20th* ─────

Remember Jesus Christ, raised from the dead, descended from David.... Here is a trustworthy saying: If we died with him, we will also live with him.   2 TIMOTHY 2.8,11

───── *21st* ─────

By his power God raised the Lord from the dead, and he will raise us also.   1 CORINTHIANS 6.14

Jesus' Resurrection Promises Victory

—— 22nd ——

The sting of death is sin, and the power of sin is the law. But thanks be to God! He gives us the victory through our Lord Jesus Christ.   1 CORINTHIANS 15.56–57

—— 23rd ——

When the perishable has been clothed with the imperishable, and the mortal with immortality, then the saying that is written will come true: "Death has been swallowed up in victory."   1 CORINTHIANS 15.54

—— 24th ——

God raised us up with Christ and seated us with him in the heavenly realms with Christ Jesus.   EPHESIANS 2.6

—— 25th ——

In baptism you were buried with [Christ] and raised with him through your faith in the power of God, who raised him from the dead.   COLOSSIANS 2.12

—— 26th ——

They tell how you turned to God from idols to serve the living and true God, and to wait for his son from heaven, whom he raised from the dead — Jesus, who rescues us from the coming wrath.   1 THESSALONIANS 1.9–10

—— 27th ——

The perishable must clothe itself with the imperishable, and the mortal with immortality.   1 CORINTHIANS 15.53

—— 28th ——

Through [Christ] you believe in God, who raised him from the dead and glorified him, and so your faith and hope are in God.   1 PETER 1.21

——— *29th* ———

Let us fix our eyes on Jesus, the author and perfector
of our faith, who for the joy set before him endured the cross.

HEBREWS 12.2

——— *30th* ———

The peace of God, which transcends all
understanding, will guard your hearts and minds in Christ Jesus.

PHILIPPIANS 4.7

MAY

Renewal

Every Christian should long to continually deepen his or her
experience of the power of the Holy Spirit. The year 1871 was a
critical one for the evangelist D.L. Moody. An intense hunger
and thirst for spiritual power were aroused in him.
Later, Moody wrote: "I thought I had power. I had the largest
congregation in Chicago and there were many conversions. I was
in a sense satisfied. There came a great hunger into my soul. I did
not know what it was. I began to cry out as I never did before. I
really felt that I did not want to live if I could not have this power
for service. I was crying all the time that God would fill me with
his Spirit. Well, one day, in the city of New York.... God revealed
himself to me, and I had such an experience of his love that I had
to ask him to stay his hand. I went to preaching again. The
sermons were not different; I did not present any new truths;
and yet hundreds were converted. I would not now be placed
back where I was before that blessed experience if you should
give me all the world."

Renewal is Promised

—— *1st* ——

"I will give them an undivided heart and put a new
spirit in them; I will remove from them their heart of stone and
give them a heart of flesh."   EZEKIEL 11.19

—— *2nd* ——

"I will pour water on the thirsty land, and streams on
the dry ground; I will pour out my Spirit on your offspring, and
my blessing on your descendants."   ISAIAH 44.3

—— *3rd* ——

"And afterwards, I will pour out my Spirit on all
people. Your sons and daughters will prophesy, your old men
will dream dreams, your young men will see visions."   JOEL 2.28

—— *4th* ——

"When the Counselor comes, whom I will send to you
from the Father, the Spirit of truth who goes out from the
Father, he will testify about me."   JOHN 15.26

—— *5th* ——

"Whoever drinks the water I give him will never
thirst. Indeed, the water I give him will become in him a spring
of water welling up to everlasting life."   JOHN 4.14

—— *6th* ——

"Even on my servants, both men and women, I will
pour out my Spirit in those days.... And everyone who calls on the
name of the Lord will be saved."   JOEL 2.29,32

—— *7th* ——

"I will ask the Father, and he will give you another
Counselor, the Spirit of truth, to be with you forever."
JOHN 14.16

The Spirit's Work in a Christian

—— *8th* ——

"This is the word of the Lord to Zerubbabel: 'Not by might nor by power, but by my Spirit,' says the Lord Almighty."
ZECHARIAH 4.6

—— *9th* ——

For we were all baptized by one Spirit into one body—whether Jews or Greeks, slave or free — and we were all given the one Spirit to drink.   1 CORINTHIANS 12.13

—— *10th* ——

Those who live according to their sinful nature have their minds set on what that nature desires; but those who live in accordance with the Spirit have their minds set on what the Spirit desires.   ROMANS 8.5

—— *11th* ——

You received the Spirit who makes you sons. And by him we cry, "Abba, Father." The Spirit himself testifies with our spirit that we are God's children.   ROMANS 8. 15–16

—— *12th* ——

The Spirit helps us in our weakness. We do not know how we ought to pray, but the Spirit himself intercedes for us with groans that words cannot express.   ROMANS 8.26

—— *13th* ——

The Spirit searches all things, even the deep things of God.
1 CORINTHIANS 2.10–11

—— *14th* ——

We ourselves, who have the firstfruits of the Spirit, groan inwardly as we wait eagerly for our adoption as sons, the redemption of our bodies.   ROMANS 8.23

The Spirit Gives Spiritual Life

—— *15th* ——

"I tell you the truth, unless a man is born of water and
the Spirit, he cannot enter the kingdom of God. Flesh gives birth
to flesh, but the Spirit gives birth to spirit." JOHN 3.5–6

—— *16th* ——

The one who sows to please his sinful nature, from
that nature will reap destruction; the one who sows to please the
Spirit, from the Spirit will reap eternal life. GALATIANS 6.8

—— *17th* ——

You show that you are a letter from Christ, the result
of our ministry, written not with ink but with the Spirit of the
living God, not on tablets of stone but on tablets of human hearts.
2 CORINTHIANS 3.3

—— *18th* ——

"The Spirit gives life; the flesh counts for nothing.
The words I have spoken to you are spirit and they are life."
JOHN 6.63

—— *19th* ——

I do not venture to speak of anything except what
Christ has accomplished through me ... by the power of signs and
miracles, through the power of the Spirit. ROMANS 15.18–19

—— *20th* ——

The letter kills, but the Spirit gives life. 2 CORINTHIANS 3.6

—— *21st* ——

If the Spirit of him who raised Jesus from the dead is
living in you, he who raised Christ Jesus from the dead will also
give life to your mortal bodies through his Spirit, who lives in you.
ROMANS 8.11

The Gifts of the Spirit

——— *22nd* ———

There are different kinds of spiritual gifts, but the
same Spirit.   1 CORINTHIANS 12.4–5

——— *23rd* ———

Now to each man the manifestation of the Spirit is
given for the common good.   1 CORINTHIANS 12.7

——— *24th* ———

To one there is given through the Spirit the ability to
speak with wisdom, to another the ability to speak with
knowledge by means of the same Spirit, to another faith by the
same Spirit, to another gifts of healing by that one Spirit.
1 CORINTHIANS 12.8–9

——— *25th* ———

All these are the work of one and the same Spirit, and
he gives them to each man, just as he determines.
1 CORINTHIANS 12.11

——— *26th* ———

We have different gifts according to the grace given us.
ROMANS 12.6

——— *27th* ———

"[The Spirit of truth] will bring glory to me by taking
from what is mine and making it known to you."   JOHN 16.14

——— *28th* ———

But to each one of us grace has been given as Christ
apportioned it. This is why it says: "When he ascended on high,
he led captives in his train and gave gifts to men."
EPHESIANS 4.7–8

MAY

—— 29th ——

When the Spirit rested on [the seventy elders], they prophesied.
NUMBERS 11.25

—— 30th ——

"Whenever you are arrested and brought to trial,
... say whatever is given you at the time, for it is not you speaking,
but the Holy Spirit."   MARK 13.11

—— 31st ——

"But when he, the Spirit of truth, comes, he will guide
you into all truth."   JOHN 16.13

JUNE

Fellowship

A Christian who had stopped going to church received a visit
from his minister and they sat down in front of a blazing log fire.
The minister removed a burning log from the fire and put it on
the side of the fireplace. After the minister had said goodbye the
man came back to his fire, saw that the log had stopped burning
and put it back into the fire where it started to blaze. Then he
understood about the necessity of Christian fellowship.
Wesley's ministry had more enduring measurable results than
that of his contemporary evangelist Whitefield. Whitefield once
said: "My brother Wesley acted more wisely than I. The souls
that were awakened under his ministry he joined together in
classes, and so preserved the fruit of his labors. I failed to do this,
and as a result my people are a rope of sand."

JUNE

Fellowship with God

—— *1st* ——

"You will keep in perfect peace him whose mind is
steadfast, because he trusts in you."   ISAIAH 26.3

—— *2nd* ——

Blessed are those who have learned to acclaim you,
who walk in the light of your presence, O Lord.   PSALM 89.15

—— *3rd* ——

"Be still, and know that I am God; I will be exalted
among the nations, I will be exalted in the earth."   PSALM 46.10

—— *4th* ——

He who dwells in the shelter of the Most High will rest
in the shadow of the Almighty.   PSALM 91.1

—— *5th* ——

I will lie down and sleep in peace, for you alone,
O Lord, make me dwell in safety.   PSALM 4.8

—— *6th* ——

The life appeared; we have seen it and testify to it,
and we proclaim to you the eternal life, which was with the Father
and has appeared to us. We proclaim to you what we have seen
and heard, so that you also may have fellowship with us. And our
fellowship is with the Father and his Son, Jesus Christ.

1 JOHN 1.2–3

—— *7th* ——

My soul finds rest in God alone; my salvation comes
from him. He alone is my rock and my salvation; he is my
fortress, I shall never be shaken.   PSALM 62.1–2

JUNE

Worshiping God

—— *8th* ——

I will praise you forever for what you have done; in
your name I will hope, for your name is good. I will praise you in
the presence of your saints.   PSALM 52.9

—— *9th* ——

Ascribe to the Lord, O families of nations, ascribe to
the Lord glory and strength. Ascribe to the Lord the glory due to
his name; bring an offering and come into his courts.
PSALM 96.7–8

—— *10th* ——

Ascribe to the Lord the glory due to his name.
1 CHRONICLES 16.29,31

—— *11th* ——

"From one New Moon to another and from one
Sabbath to another, all mankind will come and bow down before
me," says the Lord.   ISAIAH 66.23

—— *12th* ——

"Fear God and give him glory, because the hour of his
judgment has come. Worship him who made the heavens, the
earth, the sea and the springs of water."   REVELATION 14.7

—— *13th* ——

They ... read from the Book of the Law of the Lord
their God for a quarter of the day, and spent another quarter in
confession and in worshiping the Lord their God.   NEHEMIAH 9.3

—— *14th* ——

"Who will not fear you, O Lord, and bring glory to
your name? For you alone are holy. All nations will come and
worship before you, for your righteous acts have been revealed."
REVELATION 15.4

Fellowship Strengthens

—— *15th* ——

Surely God is my help; the Lord is the one who sustains me.   PSALM 54.4

—— *16th* ——

Saul's son Jonathan went to David at Horesh and helped him to find strength in God.   1 SAMUEL 23.16

—— *17th* ——

An angel from heaven appeared to [Jesus] and strengthened him. And being in anguish, he prayed more earnestly, and his sweat was like drops of blood falling to the ground.   LUKE 22.43–44

—— *18th* ——

I pray that out of [the Father's] glorious riches he may strengthen you with power through his Spirit in your inner being.   EPHESIANS 3.16

—— *19th* ——

Being strengthened with all power according to his glorious might so that you may have great endurance and patience, and joyfully give thanks to the Father, who has qualified you to share in the inheritance of the saints in the kingdom of light.   COLOSSIANS 1.11–12

—— *20th* ——

Whoever turns a sinner away from his error will save him from death and cover many sins.   JAMES 5.20

—— *21st* ——

"Do not fear, for I am with you; do not be dismayed, for I am your God. I will strengthen you and help you; I will uphold you with my righteous right hand."   ISAIAH 41.10

Fellowship with God Requires a Humble Spirit

—— *22nd* ——

The sacrifices of God are a broken spirit;
a broken and a contrite heart, O God, you will not despise.

PSALM 51.17

—— *23rd* ——

Teach me your way, O Lord, and I will walk in your
truth; give me an undivided heart, that I may fear your name.

PSALM 86.11

—— *24th* ——

Let them give thanks to the Lord for his unfailing
love and his wonderful deeds for men, for he satisfies the thirsty
and fills the hungry with good things.　PSALM 107.8–9

—— *25th* ——

Humble yourselves before the Lord, and he will lift
you up.　JAMES 4.10

—— *26th* ——

From everlasting to everlasting the Lord's love is with
those who fear him, and his righteousness with their children's
children.　PSALM 103.17

—— *27th* ——

You are forgiving and good, O Lord, abounding in
love to all who call to you. Hear my prayer, O Lord; listen to my
cry for mercy.　PSALM 86.5

—— *28th* ——

"He has brought down rulers from their thrones but
has lifted up the humble. He has filled the hungry with good
things but has sent the rich away empty."　LUKE 1.52–53

JUNE

———— *29th* ————

"This is the one I esteem: he who is humble and contrite in spirit, and trembles at my word."   ISAIAH 66.2

———— *30th* ————

Praise be to the Lord, for he has heard my cry for mercy. The Lord is my strength and my shield; my heart trusts in him, and I am helped.   PSALM 28.6–7

JULY

Jesus' Promises

One man who discovered the reality of the promises of Jesus in his own life was David Livingstone. While making the descent from the central plateau to the coastal lands of Africa, David Livingstone reached one of the vital decisions of his career. He was confronted by a chief whose people had been mistreated by the Portuguese half-castes. The chief was determined to vent his spite upon Livingstone, whose skin was of a similar color. So menacing were the threats that the missionary was inclined to escape under cover of night. Then Livingstone took his Bible and read, "Go ye therefore and teach all nations, and lo, I am with you always" (Matthew 28.20). "It is," he told himself, "the word of a gentleman of the most sacred and strict honor. I will not cross furtively by night as I intended."

Next morning he prepared to cross over to the other side while a crowd of armed natives thronged about him. The whole expedition crossed over safely while Livingstone held the interest of the natives with his magnifying lens and his watch. Then he calmly said goodbye to them and paddled across the river in a canoe. Livingstone's calm confidence in God and the promises of Jesus had enabled him to master his fears in the most difficult circumstances.

JULY

Jesus' Promises Lift Us Up

—— *1st* ——

"I no longer call you servants, because a servant does not know his master's business. Instead, I have called you friends, for everything that I learned from my Father I have made known to you."   JOHN 15.15

—— *2nd* ——

"Where two or three come together in my name, there am I with them."   MATTHEW 18.20

—— *3rd* ——

"Peace I leave with you; my peace I give you. I do not give to you as the world gives. Do not let your hearts be troubled and do not be afraid."   JOHN 14.27

—— *4th* ——

"Whoever does God's will is my brother and sister and mother." MARK 3.35

—— *5th* ——

"Give, and it will be given to you. A good measure, pressed down, shaken together and running over, will be poured into your lap. For with the measure you use, it will be measured to you."   LUKE 6.38

—— *6th* ——

Those who heard this asked, "Who then can be saved?" Jesus replied, "What is impossible with men is possible with God."   LUKE 18.26–27

—— *7th* ——

"Whoever humbles himself like this child is the greatest in the kingdom of heaven."   MATTHEW 18.4

JULY

Jesus' Promises About Prayer

—— *8th* ——

"Ask and it will be given to you; seek and you will find; knock and the door will be opened to you. For everyone who asks receives; he who seeks finds; and to him who knocks, the door will be opened."   MATTHEW 7.7–8

—— *9th* ——

"If two of you on earth agree about anything you ask for, it will be done for you by my Father in heaven."
MATTHEW 18.19

—— *10th* ——

"If you believe, you will receive whatever you ask for in prayer."   MATTHEW 21.22

—— *11th* ——

"Whatever you ask in prayer, believe that you will receive it, and it will be yours."   MARK 11.24

—— *12th* ——

"If you then, though you are evil, know how to give good gifts to your children, how much more will your Father in heaven give the Holy Spirit to those who ask him!"   LUKE 11.13

—— *13th* ——

"I will do whatever you ask in my name, so that the Son may bring glory to the Father."   JOHN 14.13

—— *14th* ——

"When you stand praying, if you hold anything against anyone, forgive him, so that your Father in heaven may forgive you your sins."   MARK 11.25

Jesus' Promises Bring Inner Happiness

—— *15th* ——

"Blessed are the poor in spirit, for theirs is the kingdom of heaven."   MATTHEW 5.3

—— *16th* ——

"Blessed are those who mourn, for they will be comforted."   MATTHEW 5.4

—— *17th* ——

"Blessed are the meek, for they will inherit the earth."
MATTHEW 5.5.

—— *18th* ——

"Blessed are those who hunger and thirst for righteousness, for they will be filled."   MATTHEW 5.6

—— *19th* ——

"Blessed are the merciful, for they will be shown mercy."
MATTHEW 5.7

—— *20th* ——

"Blessed are the pure in heart, for they will see God."
MATTHEW 5.8

—— *21st* ——

"Blessed are the peacemakers, for they will be called sons of God."   MATTHEW 5.9

Jesus' Promises Give Meaning to Life

22nd

On the last and the greatest day of the Feast, Jesus
stood and said in a loud voice, "If a man is thirsty, let him come
to me and drink."   JOHN 7.37

23rd

"Come, follow me," Jesus said, "and I will make you
fishers of men."   MATTHEW 4.19

24th

"The greatest among you will be your servant. For
whoever exalts himself will be humbled, and whoever humbles
himself will be exalted."   MATTHEW 23.11–12

25th

"So do not worry, saying, 'What shall we eat?' or 'what
shall we drink?' or 'What shall we wear?' For the pagans run after
all these things, and your heavenly Father knows that you need
them. But seek first his kingdom and his righteousness, and all
these things will be given to you as well."   MATTHEW 6.31–33

26th

"Whoever finds his life will lose it, and whoever loses
his life for my sake will find it."   MATTHEW 10.39

27th

"If you forgive men when they sin against you, your
heavenly Father will also forgive you."   MATTHEW 6.14

28th

"Enter through the narrow gate. For wide is the gate
and broad is the road that leads to destruction, and many enter
through it. But small is the gate and narrow the road that leads to
life, and only a few find it."   MATTHEW 7.13–14

JULY

—— *29th* ——

"Now this is eternal life: that they may know you, the only true God, and Jesus Christ, whom you have sent." JOHN 17.3

—— *30th* ——

"The Father himself loves you because you have loved me and have believed that I came from God." JOHN 16.27

—— *31st* ——

"I have made you known to them, and will continue to make you known in order that the love you have for me may be in them and that I myself may be in them." JOHN 17.26

AUGUST

God's Refreshment

To know God's refreshment personally and daily is a good aim for every Christian to have. After all, this is also God's will for us. A major part of the Christian life does not consist in discovering new truths but in relearning old truths. Take the longest chapter in the Bible, for example, Psalm 119. It is all about how the Psalmist longed to hear God's word and to obey God's commands. Verses 9–16 are a wonderful example to us of what our attitude to God's word should be.

Perhaps one of the keys to receiving God's refreshment is to have a spiritual life that is humble and one which is constantly hungering after and seeking God. Then we will know for ourselves what the prophet Hosea was talking about in Hosea 14.5: "I will be like the dew to Israel."

AUGUST

God's Refreshment Through His Word

―――― *1st* ――――

The law of the Lord is perfect, reviving the soul. The statutes of the Lord are trustworthy, making wise the simple.
PSALM 19.7

―――― *2nd* ――――

All scripture is God-breathed and is useful for teaching, rebuking, correcting and training in righteousness, so that the man of God may be thoroughly equipped for every good work.   2 TIMOTHY 3.16–17

―――― *3rd* ――――

The word of the Lord is right and true; he is faithful in all he does.   PSALM 33.4

―――― *4th* ――――

How can a young man keep his way pure? By living according to your word.   PSALM 119.9

―――― *5th* ――――

I have hidden your word in my heart that I might not sin against you.   PSALM 119.11

―――― *6th* ――――

Your word is a lamp to my feet and a light for my path.   PSALM 119.105

―――― *7th* ――――

Open my eyes that I may see wonderful things in your law.
PSALM 119.18

God's Refreshment in His Presence

—— *8th* ——

[God] alone is my rock and my salvation; he is my
fortress, I shall not be shaken. My salvation and my honor
depend on God; he is my mighty rock, my refuge.   PSALM 62.6–7

—— *9th* ——

"I will make an everlasting covenant with them: I will
never stop doing good to them."   JEREMIAH 32.39–40

—— *10th* ——

"His master replied, 'Well done, good and faithful
servant! You have been faithful with a few things; I will put you
in charge of many things. Come and share your master's
happiness!'"   MATTHEW 25.21

—— *11th* ——

God has said, "Never will I leave you; never will I
forsake you." So we say with confidence, "The Lord is my helper;
I will not be afraid. What can man do to me?"   HEBREWS 13.5–6

—— *12th* ——

For you, O Lord, have delivered my soul from death,
my eyes from tears, my feet from stumbling, that I may walk
before the Lord in the land of the living.   PSALM 116.8–9

—— *13th* ——

Because you are my help, I sing in the shadow of your
wings. My soul clings to you; your right hand upholds me.
PSALM 63.7–8

—— *14th* ——

Find rest, O my soul, in God alone; my hope comes
from him.   PSALM 62.5

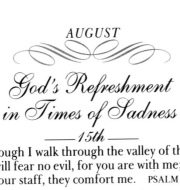

God's Refreshment in Times of Sadness

—— *15th* ——

Even though I walk through the valley of the shadow
of death, I will fear no evil, for you are with me; your rod and
your staff, they comfort me.   PSALM 23.4

—— *16th* ——

The Lord is close to the broken-hearted and saves
those who are crushed in spirit.   PSALM 34.18

—— *17th* ——

You, O Lord, keep my lamp burning; my God turns
my darkness into light.   PSALM 18.28

—— *18th* ——

Why are you downcast, O my soul? Why so disturbed
within me? Put your hope in God, for I will yet praise him, my
Savior and my God.   PSALM 42.11

—— *19th* ——

The eyes of the Lord are on those who fear him, on
those whose hope is in his unfailing love.   PSALM 33.18

—— *20th* ——

Praise to the Lord, to God our Savior, who daily bears
our burdens.   PSALM 68.19

—— *21st* ——

The Lord gives strength to his people; the Lord
blesses his people with peace.   PSALM 29.11

AUGUST

God's Refreshment in Times of Trouble

—— *22nd* ——

In the day of trouble he will keep me safe in his dwelling; he will hide me in the shelter of his tabernacle and set me high upon a rock.   PSALM 27.5

—— *23rd* ——

Cast your cares on the Lord and he will sustain you; he will never let the righteous fall.   PSALM 55.22

—— *24th* ——

The Lord is a refuge for the oppressed, a stronghold in times of trouble.   PSALM 9.9

—— *25th* ——

The Lord is my shepherd, I shall not be in want. He makes me lie down in green pastures, he leads me beside quiet waters, he restores my soul.   PSALM 23.1–3

—— *26th* ——

My flesh and my heart fail, but God is the strength of my heart and my portion for ever.   PSALM 73.26

—— *27th* ——

In my distress I called to the Lord; I cried to my God for help. From his temple he heard my voice; my cry came before him, into his ears.   PSALM 18.6

—— *28th* ——

Cast all your anxiety on [God] because he cares for you.
1 PETER 5.7

—— *29th* ——

O my Strength, I sing praise to you; you, O God, are
my fortress, my loving God.   PSALM 59.17

—— *30th* ——

"I have told you this so that my joy may be in you and
that your joy may be complete."   JOHN 15.11

—— *31st* ——

For the grace of God that brings salvation has
appeared to all men.   TITUS 2.11

SEPTEMBER

Giving Thanks to God

It's salutary to ask ourselves the following two questions. One:
What do my prayers consist of? Two: What makes me turn to
God? Many people's prayers consist of thinly disguised shopping
lists, asking God for one thing after another—for a solution to a
problem, for their family, for their own life and work. One
striking feature about many of the prayers found in the Bible is
the thread of thanksgiving that runs through them.
The apostle Paul starts off most of his letters with a short prayer
for his readers and he most often starts these prayers off on a
note of thanksgiving or praise to God. To the Romans he prays,
"First, I thank my God through Jesus Christ for all of you,
because your faith is being reported all over the world" (Romans
1.8). Paul writes in a similar way in the opening verses of
1 Corinthians (1.4–5), Ephesians (1.3), Colossinas (1.3–4) and
1 Thessalonians (1.2–3).

Thanksgiving for Life and Creation

—— *1st* ——

O Lord, our Lord, how majestic is your name in all
the earth! You have set your glory above the heavens.   PSALM 8.1

—— *2nd* ——

Worship the Lord with gladness; come before him
with joyful songs. Know that the Lord is God. It is he who made
us, and we are his; we are his people, the sheep of his pasture.
PSALM 100.2–3

—— *3rd* ——

All you have made will praise you, O Lord; your
saints will extol you.... Your kingdom is an everlasting kingdom,
and your dominion endures through all generations.
PSALM 145.10,13

—— *4th* ——

I praise you because I am fearfully and wonderfully
made; your works are wonderful, I know that full well.
PSALM 139.14

—— *5th* ——

Our help is in the name of the Lord, the Maker of
heaven and earth.   PSALM 124.8

—— *6th* ——

Every good and perfect gift is from above, coming
down from the Father of the heavenly lights, who does not
change like shifting shadows.   JAMES 1.17

—— *7th* ——

The heavens declare the glory of God; the skies
proclaim the work of his hands. Day after day they pour forth
speech; night after night they display knowledge.   PSALM 19.1–2

Thanksgiving for Specific Blessings

—— *8th* ——

From birth I was cast upon you; from my mother's
womb you have been my God.   PSALM 22.10

—— *9th* ——

Praise the Lord, O my soul, and forget not all his
benefits, who forgives all your sins and heals all your diseases,
who redeems your life from the pit and crowns you with love and
compassion, who satisfies your desires with good things so that
your youth is renewed like the eagle's.   PSALM 103.2–5

—— *10th* ——

"I tell you the truth, whoever hears my word and
believes him who sent me has eternal life and will not be
condemned; he has crossed over from death to life."   JOHN 5.24

—— *11th* ——

To the Jews who had believed him, Jesus said, "If you
hold to my teaching, you are really my disciples. Then you will
know the truth, and the truth will set you free."   JOHN 8.31–32

—— *12th* ——

"All that the Father gives me will come to me, and
whoever comes to me I will never drive away."   JOHN 6.37

—— *13th* ——

"Whoever eats my flesh and drinks my blood has
eternal life, and I will raise him up at the last day. For my flesh is
real food and my blood is real drink."   JOHN 6.54–55

—— *14th* ——

For you have been my hope, O Sovereign Lord, my
confidence since my youth. From my birth I have relied on you;
you brought me forth from my mother's womb. I will ever praise
you.   PSALM 71.5–6

Thanksgiving for Spiritual Blessings

—— *15th* ——

I have been crucified with Christ and I no longer live,
but Christ lives in me. The life I live in the body, I live by faith in
the Son of God, who loved me and gave himself for me.
GALATIANS 2.20

—— *16th* ——

I write these things to you who believe in the name of
the Son of God so that you may know that you have eternal life.
1 JOHN 5.13

—— *17th* ——

Surely his salvation is near those who fear him, that
his glory may dwell in our land. Love and faithfulness meet
together; righteousness and peace kiss each other.   PSALM 85.9–10

—— *18th* ——

The Lord God is a sun and shield; the Lord bestows
favor and honor; no good thing does he withhold from those
whose walk is blameless.   PSALM 84.11

—— *19th* ——

I am always with you; you hold me by your right
hand. You guide me with your counsel, and afterwards you will
take me into glory.   PSALM 73.23–24

—— *20th* ——

Praise be to the God and Father of our Lord Jesus
Christ, who has blessed us in the heavenly realms with every
spiritual blessing in Christ.   EPHESIANS 1.3

—— *21st* ——

He lifted me out of the slimy pit, out of the mud and
mire; he set my feet on a rock.   PSALM 40.2

Thanksgiving for God's Mercies

—— *22nd* ——

For the Lord is good and his love endures for ever;
his faithfulness continues through all generations. PSALM 100.5

—— *23rd* ——

As you know, we consider blessed those who have
persevered. You have heard of Job's perseverance and have seen
what the Lord finally brought about. The Lord is full of
compassion and mercy. JAMES 5.11

—— *24th* ——

And in their prayers for you their hearts will go out to
you, because of the surpassing grace God has given you. Thanks
be to God for his indescribable gift! 2 CORINTHIANS 9.14–15

—— *25th* ——

Praise the Lord, all you nations; extol him, all you
peoples. For great is his love towards us, and the faithfulness of
the Lord endures for ever. Praise the Lord. PSALM 117.1–2

—— *26th* ——

Blessed is the man who perseveres under trial,
because when he has stood the test, he will receive the victor's
crown, the life God has promised to those who love him.
JAMES 1.12

—— *27th* ——

O Israel, put your hope in the Lord, for with the Lord
is unfailing love and with him is full redemption. He himself will
redeem Israel from all their sins. PSALM 130.7–8

—— *28th* ——

You, O Lord, are a compassionate and gracious God,
slow to anger, abounding in love and faithfulness. PSALM 86.15

SEPTEMBER

—————— *29th* ——————

"A time is coming and has now come when the true worshipers will worship the Father in spirit and truth, for they are the kind of worshipers the Father seeks. God is spirit, and his worshipers must worship in spirit and in truth."   JOHN 4.23–24

—————— *30th* ——————

You were washed, you were sanctified, you were justified in the name of the Lord Jesus Christ and by the Spirit of our God.
1 CORINTHIANS 6.11

Bearing Fruit

The classic passage in the Bible about fruitfulness comes in John 15.1–10. Jesus Christ pictures his Father as the divine gardener and himself as the vine. In a very simple analogy Jesus Christ says that his followers must abide in him, as branches abide in the vine, in order to be fruitful:

"I am the true vine and my Father is the gardener. He cuts off every branch in me that bears no fruit, while every branch that does bear fruit he trims clean so that it will be even more fruitful. You are already clean because of the word I have spoken to you. Remain in me, and I will remain in you. No branch can bear fruit by itself; it must remain in the vine. Neither can you bear fruit unless you remain in me. I am the vine; you are the branches. If a man remains in me and I in him, he will bear much fruit; apart from me you can do nothing."

We naturally prefer not to think about the opposite to fruitfulness. However, Jesus Christ did not skate over the very real possibility of Christians falling away and in verse six he warns, "If anyone does not remain in me, he is like a branch that is thrown away and withers; such branches are picked up, thrown into the fire and burned."

Jesus Christ also homed in on the great privileges that he gives to those who are fruitful. He promises (verses 7 and 8) that they will bear much fruit: "If you remain in me and my words remain in you, ask whatever you wish, and it will be given you. This is to my Father's glory, that you bear much fruit, showing yourselves to be my disciples."

Bearing Fruit with the Divine Gardener

—— *1st* ——

"I am the true vine and my Father is the gardener."
JOHN 15.1

—— *2nd* ——

"He cuts off every branch in me that bears no fruit,
while every branch that does bear fruit he trims clean so that it
will be even more fruitful." JOHN 15.2

—— *3rd* ——

"Remain in me, and I will remain in you. No branch
can bear fruit by itself; it must remain in the vine. Neither can
you bear fruit unless you remain in me." JOHN 15.4

—— *4th* ——

"This is to my Father's glory, that you bear much
fruit, showing yourselves to be my disciples." JOHN 15.8

—— *5th* ——

"You did not choose me, but I chose you to go and
bear fruit—fruit that will last. Then the Father will give you
whatever you ask in my name." JOHN 15.16

—— *6th* ——

It is God who works in you to will and do what pleases
him. 2.13

—— *7th* ——

We pray ... that you may live a life worthy of the Lord
and may please him in every way: bearing fruit in every good
work, growing in the knowledge of God. COLOSSIANS 1.10

Bearing Fruit—Love

—— *8th* ——

Dear friends, let us love one another, for love comes
from God. Everyone who loves has been born of God and
knows God.   1 JOHN 4.7

—— *9th* ——

And this is my prayer: that your love may abound
more and more in knowledge and depth of insight, so that you
may be able to discern what is best and may be pure and
blameless until the day of Christ.   PHILIPPIANS 1.9–10

—— *10th* ——

For in Christ Jesus ... the only thing that counts is
faith expressing itself through love.   GALATIANS 5.6

—— *11th* ——

If you have any encouragement from being united
with Christ, if any comfort from his love, if any fellowship with
the Spirit, if any tenderness and compassion, then make my joy
complete by being like-minded, having the same love, being one
in spirit and purpose.   PHILIPPIANS 2.1–2

—— *12th* ——

Serve one another in love. The entire law is
summed up in a single command: "Love your neighbor as
yourself."   GALATIANS 5.14

—— *13th* ——

"All men will know that you are my disciples if you
love one another."   JOHN 13.35

—— *14th* ——

And this is love: that we live in obedience to his
commands. As you have heard from the beginning, his
command is that you live a life of love.   2 JOHN 6

Bearing Fruit—
Joy, Peace, Patience, Kindness

—— *15th* ——

The fruit of the Spirit is love, joy, peace, patience,
kindness, goodness, faithfulness, gentleness and self-control.
Against such things there is no law.   GALATIANS 5.22–23

—— *16th* ——

Light is shed on the righteous and joy on the upright in heart.
PSALM 97.11

—— *17th* ——

For the kingdom of God is not a matter of eating and
drinking, but of righteousness, peace and joy in the Holy Spirit.
ROMANS 14.17

—— *18th* ——

"Peace I leave with you; my peace I give to you."   JOHN 14.27

—— *19th* ——

Aim for perfection, listen to my appeal, be of one
mind, live in peace. And the God of love and peace will be
with you.   2 CORINTHIANS 13.11

—— *20th* ——

Peacemakers who sow in peace raise a harvest of
righteousness.   JAMES 3.18

—— *21st* ——

We do not want you to become lazy, but to imitate
those who through faith and patience inherit what has been
promised.   HEBREWS 6.12

Bearing Fruit—Goodness, Faithfulness, Gentleness, Self-control

—— *22nd* ——

Make every effort to add to your faith goodness;
and to goodness, knowledge.   2 PETER 1.5

—— *23rd* ——

[Make every effort to add] to knowledge,
self-control; and to self-control, perseverance; and to
perseverance, godliness.   2 PETER 1.6

—— *24th* ——

For if you possess these qualities in increasing
measure, they will keep you from being ineffective and
unproductive in your knowledge of our Lord Jesus Christ.
2 PETER 1.8

—— *25th* ——

I myself am convinced, my brothers, that you
yourselves are full of goodness, complete in knowledge and
competent to instruct one another.   ROMANS 15.14

—— *26th* ——

Live as children of light (for the fruit of light consists
in all goodness, righteousness and truth) and find out what
pleases the Lord.   EPHESIANS 5.8–10

—— *27th* ——

Let your gentleness be evident to all.   PHILIPPIANS 4.5

—— *28th* ——

But you, man of God, flee from all this, and pursue
righteousness, godliness, faith, love, endurance and gentleness.
1 TIMOTHY 6.11

—— *29th* ——

Therefore, as God's chosen people, holy and dearly
loved, clothe yourselves with compassion, kindness, humility,
gentleness and patience. Bear with one another.

COLOSSIANS 3.12–13

—— *30th* ——

You are all sons of the light and sons of the day. We
do not belong to the night or to the darkness. Let us not be like
others who are asleep, but let us be alert and self-controlled.

1 THESSALONIANS 5.5–6

—— *31st* ——

They will still bear fruit in old age, they will stay fresh
and green, proclaiming, "The Lord is upright; he is my Rock,
and there is no wickedness in him."   PSALM 92.14–15

NOVEMBER

Jesus' Second Coming

Johann Kepler discovered the exact laws which govern the
movements of the planets (and spacecraft). For eight years he
conducted nineteen experiments. Working on his twentieth
hypothesis, he discovered that the planets move not in a circle but
in an ellipse round two foci. The Christian life is also an ellipse
around two foci. One focus is the death of Jesus Christ on the
cross; the other is his return. Our lives need to revolve round
both these if we are to live true and effective Christian lives.
Lord Shaftesbury said, 'I do not think that in the last forty years
I have lived one conscious hour that was not influenced by the
thought of our Lord's return.'

NOVEMBER

Jesus' Second Coming Makes Sense of History

—— *1st* ——

Then the lawless one will be revealed, whom the
Lord Jesus will overthrow with the breath of his mouth and
destroy by the splendor of his coming.   2 THESSALONIANS 2.8

—— *2nd* ——

Be patient, then, brothers, until the Lord's coming.   JAMES 5.7

—— *3rd* ——

The day of the Lord will come like a thief. The
heavens will disappear with a roar; the elements will be destroyed
by fire, and the earth and everything in it will be laid bare.
2 PETER 3.10

—— *4th* ——

"Whoever practises and teaches these commands will
be called great in the kingdom of heaven."   MATTHEW 5.19

—— *5th* ——

You ought to live holy and godly lives as you look
forward to the day of God and speed its coming.   2 PETER 3.11

—— *6th* ——

In keeping with his promise we are looking forward
to a new heaven and a new earth, the home of righteousness.
2 PETER 3.13

—— *7th* ——

See how the farmer waits for the land to yield its
valuable crop and how patient he is for the fall and spring rains.
You too, be patient and stand firm, because the Lord's coming is
near.   JAMES 5.7–8

NOVEMBER

Jesus' Second Coming is Assured

—— *8th* ——

"They will see the Son of Man coming on the clouds
of the sky, with power and great glory."   MATTHEW 24.30

—— *9th* ——

For what is our hope, our joy, or the crown in which
we will glory in the presence of our Lord Jesus Christ when he
comes? Is it not you? Indeed, you are our glory and joy.
1 THESSALONIANS 2.19–20

—— *10th* ——

We believe that Jesus died and rose again and so we
believe that God will bring with Jesus those who sleep in him.
1 THESSALONIANS 4.14

—— *11th* ——

May God himself, the God of peace, sanctify you
through and through. May your whole spirit, soul and body be
kept blameless at the coming of our Lord Jesus Christ.
1 THESSALONIANS 5.23

—— *12th* ——

But our citizenship is in heaven. And we eagerly await
a Savior from there, the Lord Jesus Christ.   PHILIPPIANS 3.20

—— *13th* ——

"Therefore keep watch, because you do not know on
what day your Lord will come.... So you must also be ready,
because the Son of Man will come at an hour when you do not
expect it."   MATTHEW 24.42,44

—— *14th* ——

Now, brothers, about times and dates we do not need
to write to you, for you know very well that the day of the Lord
will come like a thief in the night.   1 THESSALONIANS 5:1–2

Jesus' Second Coming Brings Comfort

—— 15th ——

According to the Lord's own word, we tell you that we who are still alive, who are left till the coming of the Lord, will certainly not precede those who have fallen asleep.

1 THESSALONIANS 4.15

—— 16th ——

For the Lord himself will come down from heaven, with a loud command, with the voice of the archangel and with the trumpet call of God, and the dead in Christ will rise first.

1 THESSALONIANS 4.16

—— 17th ——

After that, we who are still alive and are left will be caught up with them in the clouds to meet the Lord in the air.

1 THESSALONIANS 4.17

—— 18th ——

And so we will be with the Lord forever. Therefore encourage each other with these words.   1 THESSALONIANS 4.17–18

—— 19th ——

For as in Adam all die, so in Christ all will be made alive.

1 CORINTHIANS 15.22

—— 20th ——

Therefore you do not lack any spiritual gift as you eagerly wait for our Lord Jesus Christ to be revealed.

1 CORINTHIANS 1.7

—— 21st ——

He will keep you strong to the end, so that you will be blameless on the day of our Lord Jesus Christ.   1 CORINTHIANS 1.8

Jesus' Second Coming and Heaven

—— *22nd* ——

The Lord Jesus Christ ... will transform our lowly
bodies so that they will be like his glorious body.
PHILIPPIANS 3.20–21

—— *23rd* ——

Now there is in store for me the crown of
righteousness, which the Lord, the righteous Judge, will award
to me on that day, and not only to me, but also to all who have
longed for his appearing.   2 TIMOTHY 4.7–8

—— *24th* ——

We wait for the blessed hope, the glorious appearing
of our great God and Savior, Jesus Christ.   TITUS 2.13

—— *25th* ——

"Do not rejoice that the spirits submit to you, but
rejoice that your names are recorded in heaven."   LUKE 10.20

—— *26th* ——

I heard a loud voice from the throne saying,
"Now the dwelling of God is with men, and he will live with them.
They will be his people, and God himself will be with them and
be their God."   REVELATION 21.3

—— *27th* ——

"I am the Alpha and the Omega, the Beginning and
the End. To him who is thirsty I will give to drink without cost
from the spring of the water of life. He who overcomes will
inherit all this."   REVELATION 21.1,6,7

—— *28th* ——

They will not need the light of a lamp or the light of
the sun, for the Lord God will give them light. And they will reign
for ever and ever.   REVELATION 22.5

———— *29th* ————

Be faithful, even to the point of death, and I will give
you the crown of life.   REVELATION 2.10

———— *30th* ————

Through our Lord Jesus Christ ... we have gained
access by faith into this grace in which we now stand. And we
rejoice in the hope of the glory of God.   ROMANS 5.1–2

DECEMBER

Jesus' First Coming

The evangelist Matthew wrote his Gospel so that his readers
would understand God's message behind Jesus' coming, life,
death and resurrection. In Matthew chapter one, Matthew takes
great care to point out what the real meaning about Jesus' first
coming is. He states, "An angel of the Lord appeared to Joseph
in a dream and said, 'Joseph son of David, do not be afraid to take
Mary home as your wife, because what is conceived in her is from
the Holy Spirit. She will give birth to a son, and you are to give
him the name Jesus, because he will save his people from their
sins.'"
Jesus' actual name means "God saves." He came as the Savior of
the world.

Prophecies about Jesus' Birth, Life and Death

—— *1st* ——

"But you, Bethlehem Ephrathah, ... out of you will come for me one who will be ruler over Israel."   MICAH 5.2

—— *2nd* ——

"Therefore the Lord himself will give you a sign:
The virgin will be with child and will give birth to a son, and will call him Immanuel."   ISAIAH 7.14

—— *3rd* ——

For to us a child is born, to us a son is given, and the government will be on his shoulders. And he will be called Wonderful Counselor, Mighty God, Everlasting Father, Prince of Peace.   ISAIAH 9.6

—— *4th* ——

Simeon ... said to Mary: "This child is destined to cause the falling and rising of many in Israel."   LUKE 2.34

—— *5th* ——

"The Spirit of the Lord is on me; therefore he has anointed me to preach good news to the poor."   LUKE 4.18

—— *6th* ——

He was pierced for our transgressions, he was crushed for our iniquities.... He was assigned a grave with the wicked, and with the rich in his death.   ISAIAH 53.5,9

—— *7th* ——

He poured out his life unto death, and was numbered with the transgressors. For he bore the sin of many, and made intercession for the transgressors.   ISAIAH 53.12

DECEMBER

Jesus is With Us

—— 8th ——

All this took place to fulfill what the Lord had said
through the prophet: "The virgin will be with child and will give
birth to a son, and they will call him Immanuel", which means,
"God with us." MATTHEW 1.22–23

—— 9th ——

"Whoever accepts anyone I send accepts me; and
whoever accepts me accepts the one who sent me." JOHN 13.20

—— 10th ——

"Therefore go and make disciples of all nations,
baptizing them in the name of the Father and of the Son and of
the Holy Spirit, and teaching them to obey everything I have
commanded you. And surely I will be with you always, to the very
end of the age." MATTHEW 28.19–20

—— 11th ——

"If anyone loves me, he will obey my teaching. My
Father will love him, and we will come to him and make our home
with him." JOHN 14.23

—— 12th ——

"Take my yoke upon you and learn from me, for I am
gentle and humble in heart, and you will find rest for your souls.
For my yoke is easy and my burden is light." MATTHEW 11.29–30

—— 13th ——

"I have told you these things, so that in me you may
have peace. In this world you will have trouble. But take heart! I
have overcome the world." JOHN 16.33

—— 14th ——

"If you remain in me and my words remain in you,
ask whatever you wish, and it will be given you." JOHN 15.7

DECEMBER

Jesus is our Savior

—— *15th* ——

"[Mary] will gave birth to a son, and you are to give
him the name Jesus, because he will save his people from their
sins."   MATTHEW 1.21

—— *16th* ——

Then [Jesus] took the cup, gave thanks and offered it
to them, saying, "Drink from it, all of you. This is my blood of the
covenant, which is poured out for many for the forgiveness of
sins."   MATTHEW 26.27–28

—— *17th* ——

"I am the good shepherd; I know my sheep and my
sheep know me, just as the Father knows me and I know the
Father, and I lay down my life for the sheep."   JOHN 10.14–15

—— *18th* ——

"I did not come to judge the world, but to save it."   JOHN 12.47

—— *19th* ——

We have seen and testify that the Father has sent his
Son to be the Savior of the world.   1 JOHN 4.14

—— *20th* ——

[Paul said,] "God has brought to Israel the Savior
Jesus, as he promised."   ACTS 13.23

—— *21st* ——

"My sheep listen to my voice; I know them, and they
follow me. I give them eternal life, and they shall never perish;
no one can snatch them out of my hand."   JOHN 10.27–28

Jesus is our Light

—— *22nd* ——

"I am the light of the world. Whoever follows me will never walk in darkness, but will have the light of life."   JOHN 8.12

—— *23rd* ——

For God who said, "Let light shine out of darkness," made his light shine in our hearts to give us the light of the knowledge of the glory of God in the face of Christ.
2 CORINTHIANS 4.6

—— *24th* ——

"As long as it is day, we must do the work of him who sent me. Night is coming, when no one can work. While I am in the world, I am the light of the world."   JOHN 9.4–5

—— *25th* ——

In him was life, and that life was the light of men.   JOHN 1.4

—— *26th* ——

Jesus cried out, "When a man believes in me, he does not believe in me only, but in the one who sent me. When he looks at me, he sees the one who sent me."   JOHN 12.44–45

—— *27th* ——

"I have come into the world as a light, so that no one who believes in me should stay in darkness."   JOHN 12.46

—— *28th* ——

"Whoever lives by the truth comes into the light, so that it may be seen plainly that what he has done has been done through God."   JOHN 3.21

29th

"Put your trust in the light while you have it, so that you may become sons of light." JOHN 12.36

30th

"You are going to have the light just a little while longer. Walk while you have the light, before darkness overtakes you." JOHN 12.35

31st

"The people living in darkness have seen a great light; on those living in the land of the shadow of death a light has dawned." MATTHEW 4.16